SUFFERING

A Journey Toward Spiritual Renewal
And Healing

by
Linda L. Frisby

Copyright © 2007 by Linda L. Frisby

Suffering
A Journey Toward Spiritual Renewal And Healing
by Linda L. Frisby

Printed in the United States of America

ISBN 978-1-60477-377-4

All rights reserved solely by the author. The author guarantees all contents are original and do not infringe upon the legal rights of any other person or work. No part of this book may be reproduced in any form without the permission of the author. The views expressed in this book are not necessarily those of the publisher.

Unless otherwise indicated, Bible quotations are taken from the HOLY BIBLE, NEW INTERNATIONAL VERSION®. NIV®. Copyright © 1973, 1978, 1984 by International Bible Society. Used by permission of Zondervan.

Quotation by Dr. Elisabeth Kubler-Ross, author, is used by permission from the EKR Foundation, Scottsdale, AZ. For more information concerning the EKR Foundation you may contact www.elisabethkublerross.com or www.ekrfoundation.org.

www.xulonpress.com

ACKNOWLEDGEMENTS

"For from him and through him and to him are all things."
Romans 11:36
Any book God would ever use me to write comes solely
from the inspiration of the Holy Spirit.

Special thanks to my beloved husband, Richard.
Without your steadfast love and continued support
this book may not have been possible.

My sincerest thanks to my loving Uncle and Aunt,
Charles and Ida Gossett, who prayed me
into the body of Christ.

Thanks to my pastor, Alex N. Holloway,
whose teaching and shepherding have inspired me
to develop a greater intimacy with God.

To my three sisters, Delores A. Moser, Carole A. Stewart
and Donna M. Chappell. Thank you for encouraging me and
for believing in me all of my life.

Heartfelt thanks to all my friends for their prayers
and to my dear friend, Carrie Jones, for her encouragement
and counsel.

Thanks to my special friend, Gail Allen, for her friendship,
loyalty and prayerful support during the difficult journeys in
my life and for rejoicing with
me when God brought victory over my
afflictions and suffering.

And to all who read this book, may you find spiritual renewal
and healing as you persevere
in your intimate relationship with the Lord.

Contents

Acknowledgements v
Introduction ix
Chapter 1—SUFFERING: Daily Distress 11
Chapter 2—SUFFERING: Definition 17
Chapter 3—SUFFERING: Religious Perspectives...........21
Chapter 4—SUFFERING: What It Means To Suffer 23
Chapter 5—SUFFERING: Uses Of Suffering 27
Chapter 6—PAIN: A Problem That Won't Go Away 31
Chapter 7—WHY LORD?: So Much Suffering 37
Chapter 8—WHY ME?: Why We Suffer.........................43
Chapter 9—KNOWING GOD: A Personal
                Relationship 51
Chapter 10—BENEFITS: Can Suffering Benefit Us?.......55
Chapter 11—SUFFERING: A Matter Of Choice 63
Chapter 12—OUR RESPONSIBILITY: What
                Can We Do? 67
Chapter 13—QUESTIONS...73
Chapter 14—SCRIPTURE REFERENCES 89
Chapter 15—POETIC REFLECTIONS: Finding
                Solace In The Midst Of Pain.......................97

INTRODUCTION

This book is written about every day suffering. I realize there are people who have suffered greatly due to wars, terrorism, or great tragedy. During our journey we will examine suffering of all levels, but mostly I am speaking to those who suffer every day in their lives.

Every day there are trials that affect us whether they are great or small, significant or insignificant, heavy burdens or light. What may seem like a gigantic trial to one may, in fact, become an insignificant trial to another.

Our journey begins as we define the meaning of suffering. We will pass through other areas such as religious perspectives on sufferings. Our travels will allow us to see what it means to suffer as well as some uses of suffering.

Our itinerary will allow us to see the problem of pain that will not go away. We will make journey stops to learn why there is so much suffering and why we suffer. Along the way we will see how we can have a closer relationship with the Lord and what benefits may come from our trials and tribulations.

As we proceed you will learn that suffering is a matter of choice and what our responsibilities are regarding our afflictions. Hopefully there will be opportunities for you to stop, reflect and respond to your own feelings as you develop a greater understanding of your particular situation and how to deal with it.

Our journey will be taking us toward a more intimate relationship with God. It will be a journey toward our own spiritual renewal and healing. Let us embark on our journey now.

1

SUFFERING

DAILY DISTRESS

—⁂—

The ultimate measure of a man is not where he stands in moments of comfort and convenience, but where he stands at times of challenge and controversy.
Martin Luther King Jr.
(1929-1968)
Strength To Love, 1963

Suffering is probably the most constant opponent we could have in our lives. As we journey through life, suffering can attack us in our minds, spirit and in our physical bodies. The very degree of our suffering varies. However, there is not one among us who does not, has not, or will not suffer during our life.

We would be deceiving ourselves if we did not recognize that in our every day lives we go through trials and suffering. We may suffer much or we may suffer little. But we all suffer.

Not all of us learn and benefit from suffering — that's where free will comes in — we choose how to respond. Just about every human being can reflect on his past and say they've learned from their hardships.

There are many reasons for suffering, and most certainly there are numerous benefits of suffering. Suffering may come in the form of sickness, heartache and death, a broken home or broken relationship, loss of a job, fear, oppression or any of the multitudes of things in the world that can bring us to the experience of suffering. It may fashion itself in the form of emotional hurts, everyday unsolved opportunities or verbal abuse. Its disguise may be an impetuous disaster from the past.

I have found no place in the Bible that teaches that a Christian on earth is *immune* to suffering. We are often delivered, but never *immune*. The Bible does, however, say that our sufferings, our burdens, in this world are *"light,"* literally, in the Greek, *"easy as a feather,"* compared with the glory that shall be revealed in us.

Romans 8:18 says that our present sufferings are not worth comparing with the glory that will be revealed in us. In the Bible Peter speaks of how we should rejoice though we are grieved by various trials.

We know that suffering and sickness is *not* the work of God. It is good for us to suffer because it keeps us from depending upon ourselves. It helps the church overall, and brings unity to the body of Christ. We have been commanded to give thanks in all things, even when we suffer.

God's word will never fail us, and victory will come in God's timing. While there are situations in our lives that we may or may not have control over, God is the only one who can truly bring an end to our constant struggle with pain and suffering.

Revealing my innermost feelings has never been easy for me. I have had many difficulties being open to others regarding my emotional hurts. Through the years as I have learned to share my heart with God and through my own healing process He has allowed me to be more open with people.

My journey of suffering began at a very early age. As early as I can remember my father's job required him to be away from home a few days a week, leaving my mother to care for four children. She suffered with bipolar disorder, but was not diagnosed until she was much older and the children were grown. By that time I had become an adult. Her mood swings and hurtful words were quite disturbing to me as a little girl.

When my father was not there she used me as the target of her anger and rage resulting from her manic episodes. My older siblings seemed to be spared from most of her profanation. Being the youngest it seemed I was usually the target of her anger.

She stayed in bed most of the time during her depressed times and, as I recall, did not have much interest in me. I do not believe she realized how much she was suffering. In my memory it seemed in those days most people did not display a great deal of joy due to the ambiance of the post-war years.

Since I did not fully understand the reasons for my mother's behavior, every time she said a harsh word to me it hurt me severely. I held the hurt deep inside my being. To a small child words can wound severely, especially when a mother screams "I wish you were never born," or "Go away. I do not want you around me."

I do not have recollections of ever being physically abused, but the heart wrenching words that were frequently spoken to me left long-lasting scars in my heart and mind. As a child and teen I felt very unloved and unwanted.

I did everything I knew to do to try to win the affection and approval of others. I would even strive for perfection in order to please people. Then I found that neither was I able to please those around me, I could not even please myself.

Suffering

I could not measure up to my own expectations and that in itself is a form of suffering.

I felt pain that sometimes, to this day, does not go away. The grace of God has helped me to lighten this burden over the years.

I came to know the Lord as a teenager as a result of my friend's mother loving me and caring enough to take me to church with her. But I did not come into the realization of who I was in Christ until many years into my adulthood. Throughout my life suffering has crossed my path most consistently in the form of emotional and physical pain.

I struggled for years with depression, insecurity, loneliness, feeling unloved and worthless. The childhood hurts were buried deep within my being and in my mind the hurts would frequently resurface.

The driving force behind my suffering also came through broken relationships, mental abuse, physical injury, and non life-threatening sickness, and, yes, the emotional pain. I suffered with chronic depression since I was a small child. However, it matters little the specific manifestation of my pain but rather the recognition of it. Once we learn to recognize the underlying causes of our demise, it is then we can allow the Lord to begin His healing process.

Suffering that has impacted me the most came in the form of chronic physical pain which I continue to struggle with. I suffer pain, constant pain, even as I write this in the early hours of the morning when I cannot sleep.

The damaging effects of injuries from several automobile accidents and a work related injury have left me with chronic spinal problems, degenerative disc disease and arthritis; not extremely serious problems but pain that is always present in my life.

I have had back surgery and neck surgery and I suffer with chronic headaches and neck pain. The constantly nagging pain wears on my nerves and has, at times, affected my attitude. My pain is not excruciating but can be extremely trying. It has become commonplace in my life. It is the type of pain that you eventually become immune to, but always reminding you that you hurt. It is discomforting in that it sometimes keeps me from going about my daily routine; nagging enough that my daily living can be less than pleasant. The quality of life I have is less than optimal.

In my conversations with the Lord, sometimes I have been angry, screaming and yelling to Him about my pain. Other times I have asked if I must suffer, to let it be for His glory and to please bless me, as He blessed Job in his latter days. He is doing that, and I praise Him for it. It has been a struggle, an uphill battle, but I have learned to draw more from God and his love and wisdom each day.

Realizing there are multitudes of people who suffer much more than me, the Almighty One, the Healer of Healers, The Great Physician, has inspired me to pen this book. It is written to define suffering and to show you how to overcome it.

While we may not become totally exempt from our daily sufferings we will learn what God says about the suffering we endure and what we can do to develop a closer relationship with the Lord.

I believe in our struggles we all desire to become over comers and to live a victorious life. As for me, I have not totally and completely overcome my sufferings. My burdens become much lighter each day, but my suffering will not become totally eradicated until the day I meet the Lord in Heaven.

In the following pages we will delve into the areas of the meaning of pain; the religious perspectives of pain; coping with chronic pain; how we react to chronic pain; reasons for suffering; and our responsibilities to those who suffer.

We will learn how to stay close to God during our trials and how to bear up under our trials that don't seem to go away. We will learn how we can live victoriously as we persevere toward spiritual renewal and healing.

There will be occasions for you to make *"journey stops"* to reflect upon your own circumstances, thoughts, and feelings. As you examine yourself be honest with yourself and be honest with God. This will give you an opportunity to persevere in your travels toward renewing *your* spirit. It will help you to promote your healing process.

2

SUFFERING

DEFINITION

Suffering, or pain in the sense, is basic effective experience of unpleasantness and aversion associated with harm or threat of harm in an individual. It constitutes the negative basis of affective states (emotion, feelings, moods, sentiments), while pleasure or happiness constitutes the positive basis. Whew! That is a lot to absorb.

Allow me explain it this way. Suffering may be called *physical* or *mental*, depending on whether it is linked primarily to a body process or a mind process.

Physical pain can be termed as an unpleasant sensory and emotional experience associated with actual or potential tissue damage, or described in terms of such damage. It is a sensation transmitted from sensory nerves through the spinal cord and to the sensory area of the cerebrum, where the sensation is perceived.

Examples of physical suffering are pain, nausea, breathlessness, and itching, various feelings of sickness, weakness, and certain kinds of itching, tickling, tingling, and numbness. I'm sure we all have had this type of suffering at some time in our lives.

Examples of mental suffering include anxiety, grief, hatred, depression or sadness, disgust, irritation, anger, rage, jealousy, envy, panic, frustration, craving or yearning, heartbreak, anguish, shame, sense of injustice or righteous indignation, guilt, remorse, emptiness, pity, homesickness, loneliness, rejection, and boredom.

You see, from the definitions above we all can relate to suffering of some form. The intensity of suffering comes in all degrees, from the trifling mild to the unspeakably insufferable. Factors of duration and frequency of occurrence are often considered along with that of intensity.

JOURNEY STOP!

At this *"journey stop" consider any mental or physical areas of distress you are presently experiencing. Use the space below to write your thoughts.*

People's attitudes toward suffering may vary greatly according to how much they deem it as light or severe, avoidable or unavoidable, useful or useless, of little or of great consequence, deserved or undeserved, chosen or unwanted, acceptable or unacceptable.

Many times my attitude has been less than desirable as I have responded to the emotional or physical pain occurring in my daily life. I have not displayed a positive demeanor throughout my trials.

The words pain and suffering can be confusing and may require careful handling. Sometimes they are synonymous and interchangeable. Sometimes they are used in contradistinction to one another; e.g. "pain is inevitable, suffering is optional", or "pain is physical, suffering is mental". Sometimes one word refers to a variety of that to which the other refers: e.g. "pain is physical suffering", or "suffering is severe physical or mental pain".

As I stated previously, all sentiment beings suffer during their lives, in diverse manners, and often quite dramatically. No field of human activity deals with the whole subject of suffering, but many are concerned with its nature and processes, its origin and causes, its meaning and significance, its related social, personal, and cultural behaviors, its remedies, management, and uses.

I'm just an ordinary person with every day trials. To me it doesn't matter how great or small these trials are. I am still required to make life choices daily in my response to my sufferings.

JOURNEY STOP!

As you peruse your life can you think of some great or small trials you've gone through in the past? Write down your reflections.

3

SUFFERING

RELIGIOUS PERSPECTIVES

In this book we will explore the Christian beliefs of and responses to suffering. We will look at other religious perspectives on suffering as well. We will not examine them in detail but I make mention of others' beliefs when it comes to the problem of suffering.

Suffering plays an important role in most religions, regarding matters like consolation or relief, moral conduct (do no harm, help the afflicted), spiritual advancement (penance), and ultimate destiny (salvation, damnation, hell).

Theology deals with the problem of evil, which is the difficulty of reconciling an omnipotent and benevolent god with evil. People often consider that the worst form of evil consists in extreme suffering, especially in innocent children or in beings created ultimately for being tormented without end.

The Four Noble Truths of Buddhism are about dukkha (sorrow, pain, affliction, frustration, anxiety, misery), a term usually translated as suffering. The Four Noble Truths state

(1) the nature of suffering, (2) its cause, (3) its cessation, and (4) the way leading to its cessation (which is the Noble Eightfold Path).

Buddhism considers liberation from suffering as basic for leading a holy life and attaining nirvana (freedom from all worries, troubles, fabrications, complexes, and ideas).

Hinduism holds that suffering follows naturally from personal negative behaviors in one's current life or in a past life. One must accept suffering as a just consequence and as an opportunity for spiritual progress. Thus the soul or true self, which is eternally free of any suffering, may come to manifest itself in the person, who then achieves liberation. Abstinence from causing pain or harm to other beings is a central tenet of Hinduism.

Pope John Paul II wrote "On the Christian Meaning of Human Suffering". This meaning revolves around the notion of redemptive suffering which is the Roman Catholic belief that human suffering, when accepted and offered up in union with the Passion of Jesus, can remit the just punishment for one's sins or for the sins of another.

Like an indulgence, redemptive suffering does not gain the individual *forgiveness* for their sin; forgiveness results from God's grace, freely given through Christ, which cannot be earned. After one's sins are forgiven, the individual's suffering can reduce the *penalty* due for sin.

The Bible's Book of Job reflects on the nature and meaning of suffering. The Book of Job has been called the most difficult book of the Bible. The numerous exegeses (extensive and critical interpretations) of the Book of Job are classic attempts to reconcile the co-existence of evil and God and address the problem of evil. Scholars have always been divided as to the origin, intent, and meaning of the book.

4

SUFFERING

WHAT IT MEANS TO SUFFER

We were promised sufferings. They were part of the program. We were even told, "Blessed are they that mourn."

C.S. Lewis
(1898-1963)

Now that we have explored the definitions and religious perspectives on suffering, let's determine what it actually means.

Suffering has no meaning in itself. Left to its own, it is an exasperating and bewildering burden. Given the context of a relationship, suffering suddenly has meaning.

While suffering means to endure undesirable pains and experiences, the Bible relates how people and nations experience suffering in various ways and for a variety of reasons.

Clearly an understanding of suffering introduces the problem of evil. Suffering follows the entrance of evil into the universe. Since the demise of Adam and Eve suffering has existed.

Suffering

The Bible accepts evil and suffering as givens in a fallen and sinful world. The various writers of the Bible present multiple perspectives on the causes of suffering and how it can be endured.

Several words are synonymous with the word SUFFER.

SUFFER – To submit or be forced to endure. To put up with, especially as inevitable or unavoidable. To be subject to disability.

AFFLICTION – Distress or suffering resulting from oppression or persecution. Christians often times suffer afflictions due to an injustice or persecution.

ENDURE – To bear or undergo, as pain, grief, or injury; to last, or continue to be. We must endure our trials.

BEAR – To carry burdens, to rest heavily, lean, to be able to withstand. Jesus bore our burdens on the cross.

UNDERGO – To be subjected to; have experience of; to bear up under. We will encounter suffering in our lives.

TOLERATE – To permit, put up with, bear or be capable of bearing. Sometimes we may learn to live with our afflictions.

SORROW – Deep distress or regret or a display of grief or sadness. Chronic depression, for example, may lead to periods of sorrow.

JOURNEY STOP!

Can you identify your suffering with any of these meanings? Explain.

Since suffering is such a universal motivating experience, people, when asked, can relate easily their activities to its relief and prevention: farmers, for instance, may claim that they prevent famine, artists that they take our minds off our worries, and teachers that they hand down tools for coping with life hazards. However, in aspects of collective life, suffering by itself comes often as a forefront concern.

5

SUFFERING

USES OF SUFFERING

The world is full of suffering, it is also full of overcoming it.

Helen Keller
(1880-1968)

People make use of suffering for specific social or personal purposes in many areas of human life:

Politics: infliction of suffering in war, torture, and terrorism, people may use nonphysical suffering against competitors in nonviolent power struggles; also, people point to relieving, preventing, or avenging a suffering when they want to discuss or justify a course of action.

Crime: uses of suffering for self-satisfaction, revenge or pleasure.

News media: suffering is often their raw material. It seems that most news is negative in nature.

Business: abusive demands on people or animals for profit.

Interpersonal relationships: abuse in family, school, or the workplace.

Personal conduct: in various ways, people find meaning in their lives by striving against suffering.
Sex: sadism and masochism.
Sports: suffering for performance, in training or in competition for a particular sport; no pain no gain.
Entertainment: violent video games, movies or blood sport.
For the sick, or victims, suffering may facilitate primary tertiary gain.

JOURNEY STOP!

Can you see any specific social or personal purposes for suffering in your immediate surroundings?

Even though suffering has been used for what I term "evil gain", this is not always the case. For the Christian, God uses suffering for good, such as making us stronger in our faith, leading others to the Lord, testing our endurance, and teaching us of God's mercy and grace.

Our suffering many times can affect others as they observe how we *react*, *grow*, and *learn* from our exposure to pain and suffering. What they see outwardly may adversely affect them emotionally or spiritually.

I have a friend who went through treatment for breast cancer. Although her experience facilitated some personal gain, she saw at least one loved one come to know the Lord as well.

Others in her family were spiritually awakened by what she had undergone. Some had built up their own faith as they stood with her, prayed for her, and uplifted her as she traveled through such a difficult season in her life.

The personal gain she received came as her intimate relationshp with the Lord grew. Her struggle was not an easy task. At times she did become depressed and weary, but as she humbled herself before God, He gave her wisdom, understanding and grace to help her endure her afflictions. She now has a broader outlook on life in general and has reached an entirely new realm in her walk with Jesus.

Sometimes when suffering comes, it may have no more purpose than to make us better able to assist others in their own suffering. All Christians have a responsibility to help those who are suffering. Our experiences can make other Christians strong and mature in the Lord.

JOURNEY STOP!

What are some areas in your life where God has provided an opportunity for you to assist others in their suffering?

6

PAIN

A PROBLEM THAT WON'T GO AWAY

He who learns must suffer, and, even in our sleep, pain that cannot forget falls drop by drop upon the heart until in our own despair there comes wisdom through the awful grace of God.

Aeschylus
(525 BC-456 BC)

For those who suffer pain the problem is not a theoretical problem. It is a problem of relationship. Many suffering people want to love God, but cannot see past their tears. They feel hurt and betrayed, and, sadly, the church often responds with more confusion than comfort. For many years my focus was on my pain and hurts rather than on the "Giver of Life." I had so much emotional pain I kept pushing it further down inside my being. I became withdrawn, somewhat introverted and ultimately did not enjoy life or live the joyful life I had secretly desired. I was miserable.

At one time I even became slightly reclusive. I did not want to be around people because I felt certain if I were, someone might say something that would cause my existing hurts to resurface. It surely was not my desire to have more pain in my life!

I spent many a day crying over how I was feeling and wallowing in my own self pity, instead of thanking the Lord for the many blessings He had given me.

I went through seasons in my life where I thought I had a close relationship with God. Then I would slip back into my sinful nature and become immersed in the terrible hurts inside me.

Looking back, I now see that I have lived a "see-saw" life. My walk with God had not been consistent due to the unstable decisions I had made and the struggle I carried within myself. I did not respond very well to my own suffering.

We usually think of the problem of pain being a question we ask of God, but it is also a question He asks of us. How do we respond to chronic pain?

JOURNEY STOP!

Are you focusing on your pain or on God? How have you responded to your pain?

I'm afraid my responses to suffering chronic pain were less than pleasing to God. You see, all the years of holding the hurt inside simply caused me to shut myself off from God and the multitude of good things He had for me. I hadn't yet realized He wanted only the best for me, his daughter. After all, He knew me before I was even born and while I was yet in my mother's womb. Instead of running to God I was running away from him as the evil one continued his attacks against me.

I wasn't responding to my pain in a positive way. Holding hurts and pain within oneself is not a good thing. It does not treat the problem but only causes a snowball effect, in that the hurtful words and unkind deeds had become a massive ball of hurt.

Many great philosophers have stumbled over this problem of pain and suffering. The menacing problem of pain and suffering keeps popping up despite erudite attempts to explain it away.

"The problem of pain" represents a profound riddle and the philosophers' approach to the subject sometimes takes the form of abstract reasoning, rather than looking at biblical scriptures.

For many, pain merely defines life. It is the first sensation to greet them in the morning and the last they feel before drifting off to sleep, if they could fall asleep despite the pain.

I cried myself to sleep many a night because of how the piercing negative words fired at me drove me deeper and deeper into emotional pain. I was so consumed by my own guilt and self pity that it seemed every word spoken to me fell into a bottomless well in my heart.

Then, following several automobile accidents, the physical pain came. Though I did not suffer life-threatening injuries the accidents have left me with chronic back and joint pain for many years. Living with pain has become part of my daily pattern of life.

My life seemed so overwhelming until I came to realize that my spiritual renewal came through searching out the Word of the God, making the *right* choices and developing an intimate relationship with my Savior.

Suffering

I had been confused trying to understand why Christians, in particular, suffer so much. I realize we are no more deserving than others, but I am shocked at all the suffering we are enduring.

Remember, all suffering is not severe, and all suffering is not light. Many people have given their testimonies as to how God delivered them from the most severe physical suffering. Others have testified of their deliverance from light suffering. God says in His word that He will deliver us out of all suffering.

JOURNEY STOP!

In the tablets of your memory can you see any areas where God has delivered you from your light or severe distress?

As I stated earlier, suffering occurs in various degrees. The degree our own suffering is measured by a separate and individual scale known only to each individual. In my case, afflictions have not been totally severe or extremely light, but rather constantly present.

I have had fear and anxiety concerning my particular sufferings. But I desire to replace all my fears with a strong faith, in spite of what I constantly cope with.

Still, I keep asking many questions. Is suffering God's great goof? Why, Lord, is there so much suffering? How long will all this suffering go on? What response can I give when suffering strikes, and how can I reach out to others who suffer?

JOURNEY STOP!

How have you responded when suffering has come upon you? In what ways have you reached out to others who suffer?

7

WHY LORD?

So Much Suffering
—⚏—

It is by those who have suffered that the world has been advanced.

Leo Tolstoy
(1878-1910)

God is aware of our suffering. In Exodus 3:7 the LORD said, "I have indeed seen the misery of my people in Egypt. I have heard them crying out because of their slave drivers, and I am concerned about their suffering".

God's purpose is to simplify our belief until our relationship to Him is exactly that of a child.

> **DEUTERONOMY 29:29** — The secret things belong unto the LORD our God: but those things which are revealed belong unto us and to our children for ever, that we may do all the words of this law.
> **ECCLESIASTES 7:13-14** — Consider what God has done: Who can straighten what he has made crooked? When times are good, be happy; but when

times are bad, consider: God has made the one as well as the other.

Originally, everything God made was good. Evil and suffering came as a direct result of man's rebellion against God the Creator. In Genesis God saw all that he had made, and it was very good.

After that, God tells women she will have pain in childbirth.

GENESIS 3:16 — To the woman he said, "I will greatly increase your pains in childbearing; with pain you will give birth to children. Your desire will be for your husband, and he will rule over you."

Then God said to the man that he will have to work hard all his life and then he will go back to the soil from which he was formed.

GENESIS 3:17-19 — To Adam he said, "Because you listened to your wife and ate from the tree about which I commanded you, 'You must not eat of it,' "Cursed is the ground because of you; through painful toil you will eat of it all the days of your life. It will produce thorns and thistles for you and you will eat the plants of the field. By the sweat of your brow you will eat your food until you return to the ground, since from it you were taken; for dust you are and to dust you will return."

This eliminates the idea that suffering was an essential part of creation from the beginning. You see, God does not directly *will* suffering. Occasionally, in His wisdom, God may choose to directly cause some event to occur to accomplish a greater purpose known only to Him.

Suffering

God is love. He is good and wills good. The difficulties we have are caused by natural forces, our weakness or our sin.

1 JOHN 4:16 — And so we know and rely on the love God has for us. God is love. Whoever lives in love lives in God, and God in him.

The innocent often times suffer. Paul says all creation suffered because of what man has done, and that nature groans in pain. In other words, everyone suffers because of what man in the beginning had done.

ROMANS 8:22 — We know that the whole creation has been groaning as in the pains of childbirth right up to the present time.

But there are times when suffering comes without human responsibility. In the Bible Job is a God-fearing man who experiences the loss of his family, possessions and health. It is clearly stated that Job is not being punished for his sins, but because of the malicious activity of God's ancient enemy – Satan.

There is no easy answer given in Job. Job's friends said his troubles were a result of his sinful nature. The end of the story depicts God reminding Job that he is God, and he has everything under control. Job repented and admitted he had forgotten the greatness of the sovereign God and his trust is restored.

JOB 42:5-6 — My ears had heard of you but now my eyes have seen you. Therefore I despise myself and repent in dust and ashes.

Suffering seems sometimes undeserved. I certainly have not felt I deserved all the tribulation I have gone through. The solution to that is to have confidence that through it all God is at work in us and we can know that Romans 8:28 says that all things to work together for the good of those who love God and who have been called according to His purpose.

JOURNEY STOP!

Consider areas in your own life in which you have seen God work things out for good.

For example, as I was growing older I often asked the Lord why He had not given me a mate; someone to share my life with. It had always been my heart's desire to be married and have a family of my own.

Most of my friends were married, with children, grandchildren. My three sisters were all married with families of their own. At family gatherings I always felt like I didn't fit in. I was alone and it bothered me tremendously. My life became very lonely as I seemingly always dwelled on my predicament.

I was so miserable that most of the time I would not want to go out or do things with my friends. I felt disconnected from them, like I had nothing in common with them.

No one intentionally wanted me to feel bad. Everyone tried to include me in their activities, but I was not responding to their efforts. It was the constant prodding of the evil one who planted those feelings in my mind.

Was I not pretty enough? Was I too particular in my standards for a mate? Did God not bring someone into my life because of all the hurts and pain I was dealing with? I had many questions for the Lord. I pondered why God had not honored my desire. He has a plan for my life and He works everything out in His timing.

I had not yet recognized His motive for allowing me to wait so long to find a soul mate. Was it because I was not obedient to Him? Was I not walking in complete fellowship with Him? Was I was not faithful in my walk with Him?

But for whatever reason, He chose the appropriate time to bring my husband into my life. After 57 years of singleness He did answer my prayers. He did give me the desire of my heart. You see, God is who He says He is and God does what He says He will do.

Even though I felt undeserving of my plight God was faithful to keep his word that all things *do* work together for the good of those who love him. His Word says everyone who is born of God overcomes the world. The victory that proves we are over comers is our faith. According to the Bible only he who believes that Jesus is the son of God will overcome the world.

Beloved, if you know the Lord Jesus Christ as your personal savior and as you navigate your walk of faith you can overcome any obstacle you face.

8

WHY ME?

WHY WE SUFFER

By perseverance the snail reached the ark.
Charles Spurgeon
(1834-1892)

If we are to be used by God, He will take us through a number of experiences that are not meant for us personally at all. They are designed to make us useful in His hands and to mold us as Christians, just as the clay is used in the potter's hands.

Our suffering experiences will enable us to understand what takes place in the lives of others. Because of this process we will learn compassion and will not be surprised by what comes our way.

We may not know why God takes us in a certain direction. We may not realize at the time what He is putting us through. Sometimes we go through trials more or less without understanding. Then suddenly our spirit becomes illuminated as we come to a place where God has strengthened us and we didn't even realize it.

I can tell you it is not a sin to ask "Why do I suffer so?" Many times through emotional suffering as well as my physical pain I presented that question to the Lord. Even the Lord asked this question, as he hung in agonizing pain upon the cross. Jesus was called "a man of sorrows, and acquainted with bittersweet grief".

ISAIAH 53:3 — He was despised and rejected by men, a man of sorrows, and familiar with suffering. Like one from whom men hide their faces he was despised, and we esteemed him not.

2 CORINTHIANS 1:5 — For just as the sufferings of Christ flow over into our lives, so also through Christ our comfort overflows.

JOURNEY STOP!

Have you asked the Lord why you must suffer? What do you feel was His response?

Does God cause suffering or does he allow it? Does God *want* disease? God does not want suffering or disease to exist in the sense that he enjoys it. He hates disease just as he hates all the results of sin — sorrow, death, guilt, for example.

LAMENTATIONS 3:31-33 — For men are not cast off by the Lord forever. Though he brings grief, he will show compassion, so great is his unfailing love. For he does not willingly bring affliction or grief to the children of men.

LAMENTATIONS 3:38 — Is it not from the mouth of the Most High that both calamities and good things come?

DEUTERONOMY 32:39 – "See now that I myself am He! There is no god besides me. I put to death and I bring to life, I have wounded and I will heal, and no one can deliver out of my hand."

Many times I have asked God why. However, life is still a matter of *choice* – a right choice! As God's children, and as we make the right choices, we have a promised room in our Father's own House. That is what is literally meant in John 14:6. Jesus has gone to Heaven to prepare for us a room.

JOHN 14:6 — Jesus answered, "I am the way and the truth and the life. No one comes to the Father except through me."

JAMES 1:12 — Blessed is the man who perseveres under trial, because when he has stood the test, he will receive the crown of life that God has promised to those who love him.

God must want suffering to exist in the sense that he *wills* or *chooses* for it to exist. If he didn't, I believe He would wipe it out immediately.

ROMANS 2:9 — There will be trouble and distress for every human being who does evil: first for the Jew, then for the Gentile.

PROVERBS 8:36 — But whoever fails to find me harms himself; all who hate me love death.

PROVERBS 9:12 — If you are wise, your wisdom will reward you; if you are a mocker, you alone will suffer.

If you have made a decision to accept Jesus Christ as your savior, you will never be alone. You will never suffer alone. As sure as your next breath comes, you can be certain that the Lord will be with you no matter what you are going through. Whether you are hurting emotionally or physically when you call upon the name of the Lord He will give you the grace to endure your hardships.

Once I learned to lean on God the mountainous load of suffering which was weighting me down began to lighten. It has, however, been a gradual process. Although I am still suffering today with physical pain my burdens are becoming lighter as I fully and completely place my trust and faith in the Healer of Healers.

JOURNEY STOP!

Note any burdens in your life that have been lightened or lifted by the Lord.

God chooses to allow sickness for many reasons. One of those reasons is to mold our character. In this way, God uses one form of evil, that is, sickness and suffering, to help remove another – *personal sin*.

Throughout my sickness and pain I prayed the Lord would mold my character. I asked the Lord daily to show me what I needed to learn and to reveal to me the benefits that came from my suffering. I have asked Him to draw me closer to Himself.

MICAH 7:9 — Because I have sinned against him, I will bear the LORD'S wrath, until he pleads my case and establishes my right. He will bring me out into the light; I will see his righteousness.

JOURNEY STOP!

What do you feel God's reasons were for allowing you to suffer in a particular situation?

Suffering humbles us. Trials remind us to not think too highly of our spiritual strength and test our love by how we react to them. If we genuinely love God, we will thank him for what he is accomplishing through them. I thank the Lord every day for what He has walked me through.

Suffering can be, but is not always, a penalty for our sins. Those who love God are not exempt from troubles. Although we may not be able to understand fully the pain we experience, it *can* lead us to rediscover God.

Sometimes we suffer because of the *sins of others* and not because of our own sins. It is not our fault. The Bible offers several verses that say sin will be passed down through generations.

God's promises to Abraham, Isaac and Jacob were brought to fruition as He delivered the Israelites out of the bondage of the Egyptians. Throughout the book of Exodus, we see that Moses and the Israelites spent 40 years wandering in the wilderness. His suffering prevailed over all the Israelites who were with him.

Jeremiah lashed out against the sins of his countrymen. Israel would be restored, the nations that crushed her would be annihilated, and the old covenants would be honored. God would make a new covenant with his people. He would write His law on their hearts and consecrate them to his service.

JEREMIAH 32:18 — You show love to thousands but bring the punishment for the fathers' sins into the laps of their children after them.
LEVITICUS 26:43 — For the land will be deserted by them and will enjoy its sabbaths while it lies desolate without them. They will pay for their sins because they rejected my laws and abhorred my decrees.
ROMANS 8:17 — Now if we are children, then we are heirs — heirs of God and co-heirs with Christ, if indeed we share in his sufferings in order that we may also share in his glory.

Suffering can also come to us *intentionally*. Persons who ignore the facts or refuse to take precautions can suffer purposelessly. And *unavoidable* physical suffering can come through a physical or natural disaster which can be described as an attack of Satan.

We can choose to respond negatively or in a positive way. I recall the days when my mind was filled with sadness, despair and depression. I became tired of feeling worthless and condemned, unloved and unwanted, thinking that God was somehow mad at me or He did not care for me and what I was going through. I was worn out from my constant self-examination. These feelings caused me to develop low self-esteem. Many times I was tempted to take my own life, to end all of my suffering and pain.

Sometimes I cried out to God for help. Other times I turned from Him. My negative responses did not allow me to press on in my journey. I seemed to be stuck where I was without having the tenacity to move forward.

JOURNEY STOP!

Think about your life. Were there times when you felt you were not able to continue your journey with the Lord?

Eventually I surpassed the point of self analysis. And rather than becoming bitter and angry at God over my pain and turning from him, I turned to Him. I simply fell on my face and opened up my heart to him. As the tears flowed I shared my heart with him. "You know I love you, Lord. You know the level of my faith. But this trial just keeps going on. I don't know how much longer I can endure this pain. How much more do you expect me to take?"

JOURNEY STOP!

Have you had a similar experience? If so, what would you like to say to the Lord?

I searched the scriptures for answers. I found one of my answers in the book of 1 Corinthians. God is faithful and in

Suffering

my afflictions He would not allow me to suffer more than I could bear. And surely He would provide a way out for me.

I CORINTHIANS 10:13 — No temptation has seized you except what is common to man. And God is faithful; he will not let you be tempted beyond what you can bear. But when you are tempted, he will also provide a way out so that you can stand up under it.

God knows how much we can take, and He is patiently waiting for us to ask for His help. When we walk down our winding roads of despair, we will find that His paths are straight and true. Jesus has already traveled our paths and has made our way straight.

I discovered that just at the time I thought I was at a breaking point in my life God was right there to help. He was waiting for me to ask for it. I just needed to reach out to Him. I simply said, "Father I need help. I need you. I cannot take this any more. Please hold me and ease these horrible burdens. My heart is saddened and I feel alone."

All I had to do was pray. He knows every aspect of my life. He knows when I am weak and when I am strong. Dear one, speak to Him. Get on your face before the Lord and allow Him to help you through your hard times.

JOURNEY STOP!

Remember any "God Stops" in your life when you knew absolutely that God was with you during your difficult times.

9

KNOWING GOD

A PERSONAL RELATIONSHIP

—⚏—

If we try to find lasting joy in any human relationship, it will end in vanity, something that passes like a morning cloud. The true joy of a man's life is in his relationship to God.

Oswald Chambers
(1874–1917)

There is no deeper relationship we could have than to have personal fellowship with the Lord. First we must accept Jesus as our savior. Then we are able to begin our walk with Him. He is ours. He made us. He protects us and takes special care of us.

JOHN 3:16-18 — "For God so loved the world that he gave his one and only Son, that whoever believes in him shall not perish but have eternal life. For God did not send his Son into the world to condemn the world, but to save the world through him. Whoever believes in him is not condemned, but whoever does not believe stands condemned already because he has not believed in the name of God's one and only Son.

We begin relationships at birth. When we are growing up we develop a kinship with our family, loved ones, and those around us. It takes time. No relationship is fulfilled instantaneously.

JOURNEY STOP!

How has your personal relationship with God grown from the time you accepted Him?

The Bible says we are the sons of God. What a high relationship that is, and we are privileged to hold that status. Just as our earthy father loves us and cares for us, we expect our heavenly Father to do much more.

1 JOHN 3:2 — Dear friends, now we are children of God, and what we will be has not yet been made known. But we know that when he appears, we shall be like him, for we shall see him as he is.

Abraham walked with God, as did Moses, Noah, the Jesus' disciples and many others. In their walk with the Lord each developed a distinctive communion with Him.

Perhaps in your past you have had distressing friendships with people. Whether you have been injured by others' words, had bad relationships or you are hurting because of a broken marriage, abuse, severed friendships, or a loss of a loved one, today can be your day to begin anew. Beloved, today can be the beginning of your healing process.

JOURNEY STOP!

Reflect on your past relationships. Today is your highest relationship with the Lord?

Just the deer pants for water, we should come to a "journey stop" where we know that our spirit pants after God. Our very breath comes from Him. As we journey toward spiritual renewal and healing we should behold all the beautiful things God has provided for our pleasure.

As we read God's Word, and petition Him in our prayers it is with great certainty that we will grow closer to Him. Our walk must be on a daily, and sometimes a momentary, basis.

The more time we spend with someone the more intimate we become with them. When we open our hearts to the Lord in honesty and truth our closeness to Him will bring deliverance from our bondage of suffering.

JOURNEY STOP!

Is your closeness with God growing each day as you fellowship with Him?

Suffering

We are children of God. That is easy to read, but it can be difficult to feel. Does your faith fail you today? Are you at your lowest ebb in life? What do you feel in your heart today towards God? Do you, in your spirit, have a desire for the peace and grace of God to encompass you?

Dear one, wherever you are this day, in the valley or on the mountain, God's grace is sufficient for you. As you draw unto Him, the Holy Spirit will purify your mind and divine power will refine your body.

JOURNEY STOP!

Consider your feelings toward God and your situation.

10

BENEFITS OF SUFFERING

CAN SUFFERING BENEFIT US?

—⚏—

"The world has yet to see what God will do with and for and through and in and by the man who is fully and wholly consecrated to him."

D. L. MOODY
(1837-1899)

Sometimes God disciplines us because He loves us and wants to correct us and restore us to him. He also tests us to encourage us to obey Him. Suffering can most definitely benefit us. What had I done that the Lord would correct me? Was the Lord testing me? Was it in His plan for me to develop perseverance?

JAMES 1:2-4 — Consider it pure joy, my brothers, whenever you face trials of many kinds, because you know that the testing of your faith develops perseverance. Perseverance must finish its work so that you may be mature and complete, not lacking anything.

Suffering paves the road to glory for the Christian. It proves to us that we are children of God. It is our badge of discipleship.

Suffering is used of God to purify the believer. Some suffering does comes to us from the hand of a loving heavenly Father to produce holiness and spiritual growth in us. God uses suffering to perfect us in the likeness of Christ. God purifies us until He can see the face of Jesus Christ in our lives. He refines us until the quality of our character is that of the most brilliantly cut diamond. Is the face of Jesus reflected in your countenance? Do you have a propensity to become a diamond for the Lord?

JOURNEY STOP!

Note any benefits you have seen that have come as a result of your suffering?

Because He loves us God uses suffering to chasten and discipline us to become good soldiers of the cross. God also uses these experiences in our lives to prepare us to minister in the lives of others who are suffering. Can you think of how you can minister to those who cross your path?

At the "day of judgment" glorification will be our perfect unquestionable standing before God. It is the perfection of our progressive sanctification. One day our inner character will be like that of Christ.

Suffering for Jesus Christ also enhances our Christian testimony. When we are suffering for Jesus Christ lost people will watch us carefully and listen to what we have to say.

They may even judge us on our reactions or actions to our adversities.

Early in my Christian walk I did not know how to deal with my afflictions. When I felt I was at the lowest point in my life, a place of wanting to commit suicide, I began to cry out to God and revealed to Him my feelings, disappointments, hurts, fears, and pain.

Yes, I even got angry with him. I was able to release the ugly self-destructive emotional cancer which was buried within me. That brought me to a place where God could and would reveal Himself to me. I had become transparent before Him.

I consciously made a decision to share everything with God, rather than entertain the thoughts of the evil one. Now, I'm not saying this was easy. There came a point in time (a journey stop) that it became real to me that the grace and mercy of the Lord was my only hope. I became tired of the inner struggle I was going through and I realized that the way others saw my reactions in my own sufferings would work hope for them in their times of pain and suffering.

God began teaching me how to respond to my adversities through His Word. As I began to fellowship with Him more and more the level of my comprehension of God as well as whom I am in Christ has increased.

Through the years I have learned to share with people who are going through similar experiences. This has given me insight and knowledge of how they have handled adversity. I have drawn from their wisdom and maturity in the Lord and it has helped me as I struggled with my own circumstances.

If I was reacting poorly would others see Jesus in me? As I journey toward my own spiritual renewal are others seeing me as positively responding to my trials or are they seeing a less appealing response? It has become a focus of mine that no matter where I am or who I am with Jesus would be reflected in my character.

The apostle Paul tells us his life is an example of how we are to deal with our afflictions.

1 TIMOTHY 1:16 — But for that very reason I was shown mercy so that in me, the worst of sinners, Christ Jesus might display his unlimited patience as an example for those who would believe on him and receive eternal life.

Even as I continue to walk with daily physical pain, I now realize it is the Lord who truly understands and brings comfort to me during this time in my life. He is great and all powerful. Everything I am and have belongs to Him.

I CHRONICLES 29:11 — Yours, O LORD, is the greatness and the power and the glory and the majesty and the splendor, for everything in heaven and earth is yours. Yours, O LORD, is the kingdom; you are exalted as head over all.

The key is to establish a daily walk with God. Intimate fellowship comes when one spends time with another. There is no one I would rather walk with than God. It has been my desire to have a more intimate relationship with Him and this most certainly requires discipline. We should discipline ourselves to daily pray, study the Word and walk with the Lord.

JOURNEY STOP!

Think of ways you can become more disciplined in your daily walk with the Lord.

Suffering

Are you in the middle of a dark valley of suffering? This may be your time to turn to God for understanding, endurance and deliverance.

When we know God is in control, we know that his matchless power and wonderful, marvelous grace will allow us to endure. Trusting in him brings strength and perseverance. It is in our submission to him that we learn obedience through suffering.

We must learn to live each day leaning wholly on His grace. Our deliverance may not be a sudden, instant experience, but a day-to-day walk. Walking in God's grace daily will make your burdens lighter and the healing process metamorphose. Eventually the cocoons in our lives will emerge into beautifully created butterflies.

There is *glory* in suffering. For as many of us who suffer, surely there must be great glory at the end our life's journey. Do you want to see the glory He has waiting for us?

II CORINTHIANS 4:17 — For our light and momentary troubles are achieving for us an eternal glory that far outweighs them all.

Suffering allows us to refrain from depending upon ourselves. When physical or emotional pain gets us down, we tend to ask questions of God that we might not tend to think about in our normal routine. And we tend to be open to the help of others who are obeying God.

The psalmist David cried out to the Lord numerous times in the book of Psalms. He spoke to God in prayer and in praise. He cried out to God in distress, complaints against God, in petitions, motivation for God to hear, accusations against the adversary, and in vows to praise for deliverance.

PSALM 22:1-2 – My God, my God, why have you forsaken me? Why are you so far from saving me, so far from the words of my groaning? O my God, I cry out by day, but you do not answer, by night, and am not silent.

PSALM 55:4-6 — My heart is in anguish within me; the terrors of death assail me. Fear and trembling have beset me; horror has overwhelmed me. I said, "Oh, that I had the wings of a dove! I would fly away and be at rest..."

I realize that within myself I am powerless over the torture of pain and that my only hope for refuge is in my reliance upon the Lord. I look forward to the day when sin, suffering and sorrow will all be gone.

II CORINTHIANS 1:9 — Indeed, in our hearts we felt the sentence of death. But this happened that we might not rely on ourselves but on God, who raises the dead.

Pain and suffering force us to depend on God. The wisdom of others brings us comfort. It brings us to a point of readiness to learn from a trustworthy God. Depending on God comes easy when we daily study his Word and converse with Him.

JOURNEY STOP!

How do you know you are depending on God?

Suffering

I believe once we are in heaven, the Lord will reveal all to us. We will have an eternity to have our questions answered. And once He makes it plain to us we will see how we fit into that perfect plan for our lives – orchestrated by a Loving Father who knew what it would take to keep us on our faces, moving forward in Him.

11

SUFFERING

A MATTER OF CHOICE

I believe that we are solely responsible for our choices, and we have to accept the consequences of every deed, word, and thought throughout our lifetime.

Dr. Elisabeth Kubler-Ross
(1926-2004)

Dr. Elisabeth Kubler-Ross, well known author of many books including, "Why We Are Here", "The Tunnel of Life", and "Life Lessons", quite simply gives us the answer. We are responsible for the choices we make, whether right or wrong, good or bad, and must accept our consequences for them.

There are no mistakes in life. God has a plan, a destiny for each one of us. All events in that take place in our lives are blessings so we might learn from them. But suffering requires the right response if it is to be advantageous in accomplishing God's purposes.

In my opinion, no person other than Jesus suffered so much — in so many ways, at the hands of so many people

— as did Paul. The most profound trials and sufferings are appointed to devoted servants who receive revelations from the very heart of God.

2 CORINTHIANS 6:4-10 – Rather, as servants of God we commend ourselves in every way: in great endurance; in troubles, hardships and distresses; in beatings, imprisonments and riots; in hard work, sleepless nights and hunger; in purity, understanding, patience and kindness; in the Holy Spirit and in sincere love; in truthful speech and in the power of God; with weapons of righteousness in the right hand and in the left; through glory and dishonor, bad report and good report; genuine, yet regarded as impostors; known, yet regarded as unknown; dying, and yet we live on; beaten, and yet not killed; sorrowful, yet always rejoicing; poor, yet making many rich; having nothing, and yet possessing everything.

2 CORINTHIANS 12:9-10 — Therefore I will boast all the more gladly about my weaknesses, so that Christ's power may rest on me. That is why, for Christ's sake, I delight in weaknesses, in insults, in hardships, in persecutions, in difficulties. For when I am weak, then I am strong.

If you have set your heart wholly on Christ and have determined to know him intimately, to seek Him ravenously to reveal His word to you – you are going to be set on a journey of suffering. You will experience hard times, great afflictions and deep agonies that others will know nothing about.

Now, regarding our choices, I freely admit I have "blown it" plenty of times in my life. A friend once told me when I get up in the morning I have to make a choice regarding my day. I could *choose* to be happy or sad, pleasant or grouchy, to feel good or bad. Many times I had to make a decision to simply get out of bed and face the day.

Each morning when we wake up we can even make a conscious decision to live the day for the Lord or give in to our own desires. I still blow it occasionally, but I pick myself up, ask the Lord's forgiveness and go on. Dwelling on our past decisions and choices can leave us in a situation of suffering.

I thank the Lord for biblical teachers. They reveal many wonders of faith and open up the scriptures to us. But the fact is, the revelation of Jesus Christ cannot be taught. It has to be given by the Holy Spirit. And it comes to those who shut themselves up in their own secret place, determined to know Christ. I've had to learn to get alone with God, listen to His voice and follow His path. I will leave that choice up to you.

> **JOSHUA 24:15** — But if serving the LORD seems undesirable to you, then choose for yourselves this day whom you will serve, whether the gods your forefathers served beyond the River, or the gods of the Amorites, in whose land you are living. But as for me and my household, we will serve the LORD.
>
> **DEUTERONOMY 30:19-20** — This day I call heaven and earth as witnesses against you that I have set before you life and death, blessings and curses. Now choose life, so that you and your children may live and that you may love the LORD your God, listen to his voice, and hold fast to him. For the LORD is your life, and he will give you many years in the land he swore to give to your fathers, Abraham, Isaac and Jacob.

This quality separates the two basic kinds of Christians. One kind says, "I gave my heart to Jesus". But that is all they claim regarding their faith. They do not hunger and thirst for more of the things the Lord has to offer.

The other kind says, "I gave my heart to Jesus and now I will not be satisfied until I know His heart." In other words, the servant has a fervent desire to complete his journey as Jesus walked, pleasing God as Jesus pleased God. They have a desire to know all there is to know of the Lord and to complete their journey with Him.

JOURNEY STOP!

As you examine your life which quality exhibits best your relationship with the Father?

Neither is this kind of determination something that is taught. If you truly want Jesus to give you his heart, you must be prepared to endure afflictions. The revelation of Christ you receive will be accompanied by sufferings and afflictions such as you have never known.

God has the last word in every situation. He has even overcome death.

12

OUR RESPONSIBILITY

WHAT CAN WE DO?

Unless you believe, you will not understand.
Saint Augustine
(354 AD – 430 AD)

Suffering helps the church and brings unity into the body. Our experiences and how we conduct ourselves in our suffering works hope for others. How we react in our own pain can mean the difference in victory or defeat over our personal war with pain.

Too many times, we who suffer chronic pain tend to shy away from others. We tend to revert into our own cocoon of personal torture instead of reaching out and sharing with those in the body of Christ.

However, unity comes as the body unites to support us in our afflictions, suffering and tribulations. I supported my friend with cancer through daily prayer for her and helping her with things she needed done like doctor visits and meals. I even shaved my own head when she lost her hair from the chemo treatments. God's desire was for me to be used in her life to help undergird her during her "valley experience." We are to bear (endure or carry) each other's burdens; therefore, lessening our own load.

II CORINTHIANS 1:3-7 – Praise be to the God and Father of our Lord Jesus Christ, the Father of compassion and the God of all comfort, who comforts us in all our troubles, so that we can comfort those in any trouble with the comfort we ourselves have received from God. For just as the sufferings of Christ flow over into our lives, so also through Christ our comfort overflows. If we are distressed, it is for your comfort and salvation; if we are comforted, it is for your comfort, which produces in you patient endurance of the same sufferings we suffer. And our hope for you is firm, because we know that just as you share in our sufferings, so also you share in our comfort.

GALATIONS 6:2 – Carry each other's burdens, and in this way you will fulfill the law of Christ.

As I focused on supporting my friend and lifting her up before the Lord my own afflictions seemed to become lighter. When I encouraged her my eyes were opened and my ears heard the words spoken over her. Thus, my faith was built up. I became encouraged also.

JOURNEY STOP!

Note any specific periods in your life when others have been encouraged by something you did.

The Word says faith comes by hearing and hearing comes by the Word of God. I heard myself encourage my friend and the words I spoke penetrated my spirit as well. In a sense I was speaking healing words to myself.

For those of us who have relationships in our daily lives with chronic pain sufferers we have a responsibility, not only to them, but to the Lord. We must be cautious not to ignore those who suffer chronically. We must be careful not to shrug them off or turn from them because of the constancy of their dilemmas.

HEBREWS 13:3 — Remember those in prison as if you were their fellow prisoners, and those who are mistreated as if you yourselves were suffering.

As we become sensitized to the amount of suffering in the world, we become better able to identify with what Christ suffered on the cross for us. Our character is formed when we do not rebel against the difficult times in our lives. Surrendering to God will tailor us into Christ likeness. Oh, beloved, do you have a desire to be more Christ-like?

ROMANS 8:29-30 — For those God foreknew he also predestined to be conformed to the likeness of his Son, that he might be the firstborn among many brothers. And those he predestined, he also called; those he called, he also justified; those he justified, he also glorified.

Try as we might, the many ways known to man, the only true solution to a corrupt human heart is the saving Grace of God through His Son Jesus Christ. When we, only by the grace of God, give our hearts wholeheartedly to Christ, He will give us a new heart and put a new spirit in us.

JOURNEY STOP!

Think back on your own salvation experience. Has the result of that experience changed your life?

Once you fully surrender your heart to God your spiritual healing will begin to evolve and you will find yourself soaring with Him as on eagle's wings. You will have a spiritual adventure with the Father like no other. You will find there is no one closer than God. Beloved, this will become the most exciting time in your life!

> **EZEKIEL 36:26-27** — I will give you a new heart and put a new spirit in you; I will remove from you your heart of stone and give you a heart of flesh. And I will put my Spirit in you and move you to follow my decrees and be careful to keep my laws.

While we are left in this world's system we are to *re-present* Christ. What a glorious opportunity to re-present Him! It is true that we are here to "glorify God and enjoy Him forever."

I spoke earlier about how people perceive me as I react to my adversities. I admit my past actions have been a less than pleasing representation of Christ. It is my heart's desire now that whenever my daily trials and tribulations come that I allow Jesus to shine through them. I desire to see Him glorified in all that I do.

When we learn to rejoice in tribulation, it is then that our maturity will come. As we become more like Christ, we

Suffering

---

discover our true selves, the persons we were created to be. Others will see Christ in us.

1 THESSALONIANS 1:3 — We continually remember before our God and Father your work produced by faith, your labor prompted by love, and your endurance inspired by hope in our Lord Jesus Christ.

Yes, good can come from suffering. Suffering can bring great renewal and healing. When something is for our good, Christ's glory, and to bring unity into the church, we should willingly accept it, even though it involves pain and suffering.

For, God has not abandoned us in our suffering. He does not want to see us suffer. He never abandoned me through all my trials. I abandoned Him. I did not recognize His presence in my life and that He was there all the time waiting to guide me and heal me.

His compassionate love and care will see us through our times of discipline and suffering, even when people seemingly fail us. Our focus must remain on the things of the Lord and not on others.

JOURNEY STOP!

Dear one, this is our last "Journey Stop!" Take time here to meditate on your life as a whole. Note any insights you may have had throughout your journey.

I am still being given an ever-increasing measure of grace. My faith in God continues to grow. I am being strengthened daily. My walk with Him is becoming more harmonious. In our moments of pain, Jesus will release the fullest measure of his strength to us.

I believe we all will suffer daily until our very last breath is drawn. I continue to suffer in my walk with the Lord, but each day I am making great strides toward my own spiritual healing and renewal.

We may never understand our pain, depression and discomfort, or know why our prayers for healing have not been answered. But, we really don't have to know why.

Beloved, as we journey through life there will be many great things to behold along the way. We can know that God has already answered us, "You have got my grace ... and, my beloved child that is all you need."

13

QUESTIONS

—∞—

In this chapter we will review what we have learned during our journey toward spiritual renewal and healing. You may have previously answered some of these questions but now have gained a greater insight and better understanding of your own life. Feel free to use the space provided to introduce any new observations you have viewed along the way.

Doesn't God care about me?

Of course, God cares about you. God never forgets His people. God remembered Abraham and Lot and delivered Lot out of catastrophe. He also remembered the Israelites who wandered in the wilderness for 40 years and He let them to the promise land.

God commanded Noah to build and ark for his family and a host of beasts and birds then sent a flood to destroy

Suffering

all other life. He did not forget Noah and all the animals and livestock that were with him in the ark. He sent a wind over the earth, and the waters receded.

It makes sense that after God commanded Noah to build the ark that He would deliver him from the flooded earth. When the Word says that God remembers, we can assume an action on His part.

God remembers everything and keeps all of His promises and covenants. God acts on what He remembers. He remembers the future as actively as He remembers the past. God is faithful to us. He means to be noticed and he means to be remembered. He cannot be otherwise.

Is God really my Lord?

Our joy comes from seeing the total fulfillment of the purpose for which we were created and *born again*. The only way you can say God is our Lord is to have the assurance that you have accepted Jesus as your personal savior. To do this you must acknowledge that you are a sinner, ask Him for forgiveness and ask Jesus to come into your heart.

It is not from successfully doing something of our own choosing. The joy of the Lord comes from obeying Him and from doing what He has asked us to do.

We each must find our own niche in life and spiritually we find it when we receive a ministry from Him. To do this we must have a personal relationship with God and a close fellowship with Jesus. We must know He is more than a personal savior.

Suffering

God does not offer us a choice of how we can serve Him. He asks us for complete loyalty to His commission. He wants faithfulness from us which comes as our personal relationship with Him grows. We should be sensitive to what God has called us to do.

Why do I suffer?

We often suffer because of the sins of others, and not our own sins. Joseph suffered because his brothers threw him into a well, pulled him out and sold him to the Ishmaelites.

Sometimes the suffering that comes to us is not our fault. It just happens. That is what the disciples learned as they walked with Jesus. In this case, how we react to the suffering is the key.

JOHN 9:1-3 — As he went along, he saw a man blind from birth. His disciples asked him, "Rabbi, who sinned, this man or his parents, that he was born blind?" "Neither this man nor his parents sinned," said Jesus, "but this happened so that the work of God might be displayed in his life.

Sometimes God sends suffering as punishment for our sins. He disciplines us because He loves us and wants to correct us and restore us to Him.

DEUTERONOMY 8:2 — Remember how the LORD your God led you all the way in the desert these forty years, to humble you and to test you in

Suffering

order to know what was in your heart, whether or not you would keep his commands.

Sometimes we willingly suffer because we must take a stand for Christ. Peter stated that if we are insulted because of the name of Christ, we are blessed.

Other times we willingly suffer because it will help us grow and mature. James spoke to the twelve tribes scattered among the nations. He said to consider it pure joy whenever you face trials of many kinds, because the testing of your faith develops perseverance.

The world hates Christ, so when we identify with Him, we can expect the world that inflicted suffering on Him to also inflict suffering on us. Christians are not exempt from persecution.

2 TIMOTHY 3:12 — In fact, everyone who wants to live a godly life in Christ Jesus will be persecuted.

Can any good come from suffering?

Suffering or woundedness can bring great renewal and healing. We are blessed when God corrects us. If God did not love us He would not correct us. Therefore, we should count our afflictions as blessings. God is here to heal all of our sufferings.

JOB 5:17-18 — Blessed is the man whom God corrects; so do not despise the discipline of the

Almighty. For he wounds, but he also binds up; he injures, but his hands also heal.

1 PETER 4:1-2 — Therefore, since Christ suffered in his body, arm yourselves also with the same attitude, because he who has suffered in his body is done with sin. As a result, he does not live the rest of his earthly life for evil human desires, but rather for the will of God.

When something is for our good, Christ's glory, and the building of His church, we should be happy to accept it, even though it is suffering. There is healing in joy and laughter.

We should count all of our trials as joy. We should learn to rejoice as we persevere. I cannot stress enough how important it is for we, as Christians, to give thanks to God in all things.

ROMANS 5:3-4 — Not only so, but we also rejoice in our sufferings, because we know that suffering produces perseverance; perseverance, character; and character, hope.

HEBREWS 12:11 — No discipline seems pleasant at the time, but painful. Later on, however, it produces a harvest of righteousness and peace for those who have been trained by it.

II CORINTHIANS 1:5 – For just as the sufferings of Christ flow over into our lives, so also through Christ our comfort overflows.

II CORINTHIANS 12:10 — That is why, for Christ's sake, I delight in weaknesses, in insults, in hardships, in persecutions, in difficulties. For when I am weak, then I am strong.

Why should I trust God?

We must trust in God's sovereignty over all occurrences in our lives. God is either sovereign over all or not sovereign at all!

God is not responsible for pain, but God will give us strength to help us cope. If our particular view of God is adding to our suffering rather than easing it, we may want to re-examine those beliefs.

Well known great humanitarian, pastor, and author Charles Spurgeon once said that you are a child of God and you should never forget that all of your suffering comes from the divine hand of God. You see, God's purpose in giving suffering is to strengthen our trust in him.

> **PSALM 9:9-10** — The LORD is a refuge for the oppressed, a stronghold in times of trouble. Those who know your name will trust in you, for you, LORD, have never forsaken those who seek you.
>
> **PROVERBS 3:5-6** — Trust in the LORD with all your heart and lean not on your own understanding; in all your ways acknowledge him, and he will make your paths straight.

How long will this suffering last?

Our suffering will last as long as we are on this earth. Individual seasons of suffering may last for a little while, but for the Christian suffering is almost constant. When we submit to Christ and strive to become Christ-like He will continue to prune us and mold us into His own image we will have adversity. As long as we are in His hands He will continue to hone our character and build us up in the faith. Remember, it is God who gives us the wisdom and grace to endure our afflictions.

PSALM 55:16-17 — But I call to God, and the LORD saves me. Evening, morning and noon I cry out in distress, and he hears my voice.

ISAIAH 41:10 — So do not fear, for I am with you; do not be dismayed, for I am your God. I will strengthen you and help you; I will uphold you with my righteous right hand.

ISAIAH 43:25 — I, even I, am he who blots out your transgressions, for my own sake, and remembers your sins no more.

How should I respond to my adversities?

It's going to be a struggle all the way. That's why they are called trials and tests. I struggle daily in my walk with the Lord.

Even when we understand the purposes and principles of suffering, and we know the promises of God's love and concern given in the Word of God for handling suffering, dealing with the trials of life is never easy because suffering hurts.

We should count it all joy as we recall God's perspective and purposes for trials. We should rely on God's promises in our trials, and remember to let the trial run its course as God designs and permits this for spiritual growth and maturity.

We should pray for God's wisdom to do His will and we should recognize that responding correctly to trials is worth it both in time and eternity!

PSALM 27:14 — Wait for the LORD; be strong and take heart and wait for the LORD.

PSALM 118:24 — This is the day the LORD has made; let us rejoice and be glad in it.

What is the purpose of suffering?

We must understand God's chief purpose for our lives is to be conformed to the image of Christ and he has determined in his plan to use suffering for our spiritual development. If we are going to endure suffering and the trials of life, however, we must also understand the other purposes and reasons for suffering as they are related to the chief purpose.

> **1 PETER 4:16** — However, if you suffer as a Christian, do not be ashamed, but praise God that you bear that name.
>
> **HEBREWS 12:2-3** — Let us fix our eyes on Jesus, the author and perfecter of our faith, who for the joy set before him endured the cross, scorning its shame, and sat down at the right hand of the throne of God. ³Consider him who endured such opposition from sinful men, so that you will not grow weary and lose heart.

Our freedom and faith emerge from deliberate acts of our will to shift our focus from all that differs to the glorious truth of the living God. He breaks the strongholds of our negative meditations when we *bow own* in His presence. That is when our freedom and faith can emerge.

How can God use suffering in my life?

God can use suffering in your life to hone your character and to build your faith. We all want character but we do not want the suffering that goes with it.

Suffering

When believers handle suffering joyfully and with stability, it becomes a wonderful testimony to the power and life of Christ. People who know you and view your suffering can be mightily encouraged and strengthened by your experience.

JAMES 1:12 — Blessed is the man who perseveres under trial, because when he has stood the test, he will receive the crown of life that God has promised to those who love him.

1 PETER 1:6-7 — I this you greatly rejoice, though now for a little while you may have had to suffer grief in all kinds of trials. These have come so that your faith — of greater worth than gold, which perishes even though refined by fire — may be proved genuine and may result in praise, glory and honor when Jesus Christ is revealed.

Our suffering provides key opportunities to manifest and magnify the power of God through us in order to verify and confirm the messenger and His message.

How could we, without sufferings, manifest the nature and truth of the Christian graces! What place should we then have for patience, submission, meekness, forbearance, and a readiness to forgive, if we had nothing to try us, either from the hand of the Lord, or from the hand of men!

How does my obedience to God affect other people?

If we obey God, it is going to cost others more than it costs us. That is where the pain begins. If we love the Lord, obedience does not cost us anything. It is a delight for us to love the Lord. When we obey God it sometimes upsets others' plans. Those who do not love Him may ridicule us. We must simply obey the Lord and leave all the consequences with Him.

How do I stay close to God in times of suffering?

Recognize that God has not abandoned you in times of suffering. Often times we feel that God has abandoned us, but it is we who have abandoned God. Keep your eyes on him, for he has not hidden is face from you.

> **PSALM 22:24** — For he has not despised or disdained the suffering of the afflicted one; he has not hidden his face from him but has listened to his cry for help.

Recognize that suffering is not forever. In the dark hours of the night of suffering it is difficult to think of a morning of joy and gladness. But the tears of suffering are like seeds of joy.

PSALM 126:5-6 – Those who sow tears shall reap joy. Yes, they go out weeping, carrying seed for sowing, and return singing, carrying their sheaves.

Recognize that God does not want to see us suffer. A loving God does not enjoy the disciplines of life that must come our way. But His compassionate love and care see us through our times of discipline and suffering.

LAMENTATIONS 3:32-33 — Though he brings grief, he will show compassion, so great is his unfailing love. For he does not willingly bring affliction or grief to the children of men.

Recognize that Jesus himself suffered for us. Christ suffered the agonies of the cross, which not only embraced incredible physical torture but also the unthinkable suffering of bearing the sins of the world.

LUKE 24:26 — Did not the Christ have to suffer these things and then enter his glory?"
MATTHEW 17:12 — But I tell you, Elijah has already come, and they did not recognize him, but have done to him everything they wished. In the same way the Son of Man is going to suffer at their hands."
HEBREWS 2:18 – Because he himself suffered when he was tempted, he is able to help those who are being tempted.

The real light is cast upon the problem of a suffering Christian. The most perplexing feature of that problem is

Suffering

how to harmonize our sufferings with the love of God. But if God had ceased to care for us, His children, then He had deserted them. The Divine Comforter is given to help our infirmities.

How can I bear up under my trials?

We could not, and therefore divine grace has provided for us an all-sufficient helper. Without God's aid we had long since succumbed, mastered by our trials. Our hope looks forward to the glory to come. In the weary interval of waiting, the Spirit supports our troubled hearts and grace remains alive within us.

1 CORINTHIANS 10:13 — No temptation has seized you except what is common to man. And God is faithful; he will not let you be tempted beyond what you can bear. But when you are tempted, he will also provide a way out so that you can stand up under it.

I trust you find the name and grace of Jesus more and more precious to you and his promises more fragrant. I trust your hope in them becomes more abiding; your sense of your own weakness and unworthiness daily increasing. May your persuasion of his all-sufficiency, to guide, support, and comfort you, be more confirmed in your spirit.

You owe your growth in these respects in a great measure to His blessing upon those afflictions which He has prepared for you, and sanctified to you. May you praise Him for all that is past, and trust him for all that is to come!

How should I react when suffering?

We need to understand God's attitude toward suffering. He is a Sovereign God who works all things according to His perfect wisdom and will. He does not see suffering as something evil to avoid. Rather, He harnesses it to become an instrument for our eventual good and His glory.

Suffering, in the eyes of the world is a thing of shame. Being a disciple of Jesus Christ is never something of which we should be ashamed.

What should be my attitude toward suffering?

Peter suggests a number of heart attitudes that are essential for us if we are to react properly under suffering. One is the discipline of holy living. For many years I struggled with this attitude. We are a chosen people and should abstain from sinful desires.

Another is to have a humble, surrendered heart toward Jesus, then toward others. We should humble ourselves under God's mighty hand, so that he may lift us up in His time.

We must also exercise self-control, which is also a fruit of the Spirit. There is never any occasion in our lives which warrant any other attitude than to have Christ-like humility and godly self control.

We should look forward to the assurance of our final victory and restoration. There will always be someone watching our responses to suffering. We should be ready to pass our encouragement on to others in need of the encouragement we have received.

14

SCRIPTURE REFERENCESS

Suffering From God

Suffering sometimes comes from God. Noah suffered because God chose to flood the earth. David cried out to God in his sufferings.

DEUTERONOMY 8:2
DEUTERONOMY 32: 39-42
JOB 5:17-26
JOB 7:17-18
JOB 5:17-26
PSALM 9:7-10
PSALM 22:1
PSALM 30:5
PSALM 50:21
PSALM 107:10
PSALM 119:75
PROVERBS 3:11-12
PROVERBS 17:3
ECCLESIASTES 7:13-14
ISAIAH 13:8

ISAIAH 48:10-11
ISAIAH 53:10
ISAIAH 54:7-17
LAMENTATIONS 1:1-2
LAMENTATIONS 2:5
LAMENTATIONS 3:1-6
LAMENTATIONS 3:8
LAMENTATIONS 3:31-33
LAMENTATIONS 4:8-11
HOSEA 6:1
ACTS 2:22-24
2 CORINTHIANS 7:9-11
HEBREWS 12:5-11

Suffering With God

David suffered with God as he walked through the valley of the shadow of death. He feared no evil because God was with him.

PSALM 18:5-6
PSALM 22:4-5
PSALM 22:24
PSALM 23:4
PSALM 27:1
PSALM 50:15
PSALM 55:1-3
PSALM 55:1-7
PSALM 57:1
PSALM 77:1-2
PSALM 86:6-7
PSALM 88:1-4
PSALM 113:7-8
PSALM 116:1-2
PSALM 119:50

PSALM 142:1-2
PSALM 143:9
PSALM 145:19
ISAIAH 41:10
ISAIAH 43:2-3
2 CORINTHIANS 1:3-4
1 THESSELONIANS 2:1-2

Suffering From Satan

We sometimes suffer because the temptation of Satan. As Christians we are not exempt from the enticement of sin in our daily lives.

LUKE 22:31-34
1 PETER 5:7-10

Suffering By Christ

Jesus suffered in great agony when he bore our sins on the cross. Below are some scriptures that depict how Jesus suffered.

ISAIAH 53:3
ACTS 2:22-24
ACTS 3:18-20
ACTS 9:1-5
2 CORINTHIANS 8:9
1 THESSALONIANS 5:9-10
HEBREWS 2:9-10
HEBREWS 4:14-16
HEBREWS 5:8-10
HEBREWS 9:27-28
HEBREWS 13:11-15
1 PETER 2:23-24

1 PETER 4:1-2
1 PETER 2:20-21

Suffering For Christ

The apostle Paul said he delighted in his weaknesses, difficulties, hardships, persecution and in insults because when he was weak Jesus made him strong. Below are some references to how we suffer for Christ.

JOB 23:10
MATTHEW 24:9
ROMANS 8:18
2 CORINTHIANS 12:7-10
EPHESIANS 3:13
1 TIMOTHY 3:12
1 PETER 1:6-7
1 PETER 4:16
1 PETER 4:19
ACTS 4:2-3
ACTS 5:14-18
ACTS 5:38-42
ACTS 7:51-62
ACTS 9:15-16
ACTS 9:22-26
ACTS 12:1-5
ACTS 13:50-51
ACTS 14:3-5
ACTS 14:18-20
2 CORINTHIANS 4:7-18
2 CORINTHIANS 11:22-31
HEBREWS 2:18
HEBREWS 10:32-35
HEBREWS 13:11-15

Suffering With Christ

Everyone who wants to live a godly life will suffer. Paul said we are not to be surprised at the painful trials of suffering, but to rejoice in that we participate in the sufferings of Christ.

PHILIPPIANS 3:7-11
2 TIMOTHY 3:10-12
HEBREWS 2:18
1 PETER 4:12-13

Suffering Because Due To Own Actions

We can suffer due to our own actions. Herod suffered by his own actions when he did not give praise to God and was struck down by an angel of the Lord and died.

PSALM 16:4
PSALM 107:10-14
PSALM 118:18
LAMENTATIONS 1:1-2
LAMENTATIONS 1:8-9
LAMENTATIONS 1:16, 29
LAMENTATIONS 2:11-12
LAMENTATIONS 3:47-50
LAMENTATIONS 4:12-13
LAMENTATIONS 5:10-17
MICAH 7:9
LUKE 22:31-34
ACTS 12:21-24
ACTS 13:9-11
ACTS 19:13-16
ACTS 24:11-12
EPHESIANS 1:4

Our Part Regarding Suffering

David called to the Lord in the torrents of his destruction when confronted with the snares of death. God heard his cries and delivered him. The following scriptures give us examples of our part regarding suffering.

2 CHRONICLES 20:12, 15, 18
NEHEMIAH 1:4
PSALM 18:5-6
PSALM 22:1-2
PSALM 23:1
PSALM 56:4
PSALM 27:14
PSALM 55:22
PSALM 88:8-9
PSALM 88:13-18
PSALM 77:1-2
PSALM 118:24
PSALM 119:71
PSALM 142:1-2
PSALM 143:1-2
PSALM 143:1-2
PROVERBS 17:17
PROVERBS 25:20
ECCLESIASTES 7:2-4
ECCLESIASTES 7:10
LAMENTATIONS 3:38-40
LAMENTATIONS 3:55-58
LAMENTATIONS 5:19-22
OBADIAH 12
HABAKKUK 3:17-18
MATTHEW 11:28-30
MATTHEW 25:35-46
JOHN 15:7

Suffering

ROMANS 5:3-5
ROMANS 8:35-37
ROMANS 12:12-19
1 CORINTHIANS 4:9-14
1 CORINTHIANS 8:1-5
1 CORINTHIANS 9:24-27
11 CORINTHIANS 10:24
CORINTHIANS 12:22-27
2 CORINTHIANS 4:16-17
EPHESIANS 4:1-2
PHILIPPIANS 4:19
PHILIPPIANS 4:6-7, 12
1 THESSALONIANS 5:16-18
2 THESSALONIANS 1:3-10
JAMES 1:2-4
1 PETER 2:21-22
1 PETER 4:1-2

15

POETIC REFLECTIONS

Finding Solace In The Midst Of Pain

I would like to share some of my meditations and poetry, all of which were written during seasons in my life when I was depressed and suffering. I somehow always managed to come away with encouragement and in awe of the beauty of God's creation.

SPRING

Spring is almost here.
Flowers are popping up everywhere;
The grass is growing tall and green
And happy faces everywhere can be seen.

The trees awaken from their long winter's rest;
The birds are busily building new nests.
Animals awaken from their winter's slumber;
They yawn, they're stiff, and oh, how they hunger.

'Tis a miracle that all this should happen;
That God gave us such a marvelous creation.
We are blessed to be given such magnificent beauty
To protect and enjoy, for it is surely our duty.

During this period of rest which God gives us, do not lay idly, but be in constant prayer and meditation on His word.

Lie patiently and let His cool, healing hands fall upon your soul. Lay your life's ambitions and dreams at His feet.

Do not become hurried, for He will grasp your hand and lift you up in His own time.

God is the creator of the heaven and the earth – all that is and all that is to be!

Oh, what beauty we find in today. If we only look around us we can see evidence of the wondrous things that only He could create.

Even the cold gray clouds of a dreary winter's day show the beauty of the Creator.

Much praise and thanks should be offered the Lord for giving us such wondrous beauty. If we open our eyes to Him, He will guide us out of the darkness we sometimes find ourselves in.

Spring Again

It's Spring again and suddenly I can see
Birds perched in every blooming tree.
They sing songs in harmony without a care;
Each his own part in which to share —
While colorful flowers spring up everywhere.

It's Spring and once again the pastures green
To me look so lavishly soft and velveteen.
And as I gaze upon the skies of blue
Butterflies, cardinals and blue birds, too
Suddenly appear as they make their debut.

Spring comes forth as I stand in wonder
Observing the animals awaking from their slumber.
And though sparsely scattered storm clouds I can see
These miraculous changes are still a mystery to me
As the Lord looks down and smiles at His marvelous
    feat.

    I wonder why God made the birds to sing, or fly above the ground; why some are colorful and some are drab. Why did He make each to sing a different song? How did He teach birds to build a nest or to fly southward in the winter?
    How miraculous is this great work of His, to have such beauty mingled with song.

A World Unseen

What wondrous things our God has made –
    In such lovely ways He has displayed
The simple things we take for granted,

Like trees and grass that He has planted
Spring up around us but go unnoticed.

A bird flying in the air
    As though it has no worries, no cares –
A butterfly so delicate and soft
    Upon a flower it sits aloft
In proud display of all its beauty.

Oh, how tall the flower stands
    Patiently awaiting its creator's commands –
Laughing and smiling it freely sways,
    Perhaps to brighten someone's days –
One who possibly may not have noticed.

The miracles of God's creations
    Go unseen throughout the nations
By those of us who fail to see
    That only a master such as He
Could make these things for us
    To share with our fellow man.

Today I Said A Prayer For You

Today I said a prayer for you.
The Holy Spirit had revealed to me
There might be something you are going through.
So I commanded the demons of hell to flee.

Today I said a prayer for you.
There's a special bond 'tween you and me.
I asked the Lord to guide you through
Because you are so dear to me.

Today I said a prayer for you.
I asked the Lord to give you light to see
And in the Word there are promises true
That a light unto thy path there would surely be.

Today I said a prayer for you.
The Spirit of the Lord said, "I am the way and truth, you see."
So I asked the Lord to keep watch over you
Because you're a child of His, and so special to me.

Today I said a prayer for you.
That He would meet your every need,
And keep you safe the whole day through,
So tomorrow — a brand new day — you might see.

That prayer I said today for you
Went to the throne room with love, you see,
And thanks for all you have seen me through.
And all you have meant to me.

Seasons

Winter
Winter is the period God chose to show the softness and gentleness of Heaven. He prepares His earthly creations for peace and slumber. He protects His earth by covering it with angel hair which we call snow. *Winter is heavenly!*

Spring
Spring is the time of year God chose to show the beauty of Heaven. He creates lovely flowers, beautiful trees, and gives new life to animals, birds and insects. He puts the

sweet smell in the air once again, and the beauty into the earth. *Spring is heavenly!*

Summer

Summer is when He shows us, through nature, the warmth and comfort we will receive in Heaven, as we lie down in His green pastures. We will witness no pain, no sorrow, and feel not the presence of Satan. *Summer is heavenly!*

Autumn

In Autumn God shows us the everlasting life we will receive in heaven. He shows us that we cannot quit, simply because a storm approaches. The trees lose their leaves; the grass its color; the air, its warmth from summer. These things do not quit, but rather, prepare themselves for the next phase of their lives. *Autumn is heavenly!*

You too, can see the characteristics of Heaven as I have seen. If you have the Lord in your heart, you will love Him and His creations more and more as each day passes. You will learn to appreciate life's many trials and temptations — *if you will only give yourself to Him.*

Rendezvous With Jesus

The birds happily sing at my window,
The trees sway as the Spring winds blow,
A startling sound as my alarm rings true
As I awaken to start a day that's brand new.

As others slumber in their blankets cuddled,
I spring to my feet quick as a bursting bubble.
My heart is eager to be on the road I know so well;
I have a rendezvous with Jesus – so much to tell.

We walk quietly together among the trees,
Jesus and me – laughing, sharing and enjoying the breeze
And as we come to a meadow I pause to remember
This day he has given me so regal, in all of its splendor.

Then I fall on my knees as I behold His face
In the wondrous beauty I see in this place.
The peace He brings as we journey together
Will remain in my heart forever and ever.

Then I quickly arise and turn again toward home
Only to realize that I am never alone
And that as I go about my business today
Jesus will walk beside me each step of the way.

You could also know a friend so true
If you, but open your heart and let Him in too.
He will guide you, direct you and light your path,
So why not give him the opportunity at last!

He'll meet you each morning as you arise
And be at your bedside to say "good night."
He'll rendezvous with you; greet you with a smile
Then journey beside you all of the while.

Who's Praying For Me?

Lord, when I awake each morning to begin my day
And eat my breakfast before going on my way
You quicken me to pray for others.
But, Lord, who's praying for me?

Suffering

Lord, as I follow the plans you have set before me
And busily go about performing my daily deeds
You quicken me to pray for others.
But, Lord, who's praying for me?

Lord, when I'm hurriedly driving from here to there
To attend to those you have placed in my care
You quicken me to pray for others.
But, Lord, who's praying for me?

Lord, when I rare back in my chair at evening's sun
And reflectively ponder the many things I have done
You quicken me to pray for others.
But, Lord, who's praying for me?

Lord, when I finally take to my bed to rest
And wonder if today I had done my best
You quicken me to pray for others.
But, Lord, who's praying for me?

Lord, while peacefully sleeping after my day-long
    journey
With no thoughts on my mind, no reasons to hurry
You awaken me and quicken me to pray for others.
But, Lord, who's praying for me?

Lord, again I ask you who will pray?
Who will remember me in their prayers each day?
My peers, church family, my pastor and others —
Intercessors, my friends, my loved ones, too?

Suffering

Alas, the answer you've revealed to me because you
 dare.
None will pray but those with whom I share
My needs, my desires, my trials and 'druthers —
Those you quicken, Lord, will pray,
Because you know best.

END

www.ingramcontent.com/pod-product-compliance
Lightning Source LLC
LaVergne TN
LVHW041712060526
838201LV00043B/687